cover : *Manta* desk (detail)

© Dis Voir, 2021
www.disvoir.com
www.facebook.com/groups/disvoir/

ISBN 978-2-914563-98-7

PRINTED in EUROPE

Noé Duchaufour-Lawrance

DESIGN SERIES

Pierre Paulin
Anne-Marie Fèvre, Elisabeth Védrenne

François Bauchet
Jacques Bonnaval, Claire Fayolle

Luigi Colani
Philippe Pernodet, Bruce Mehly

Petits Enfants de Starck
(Beef, Matali Crasset, Jean-Marie Massaud, Patrick Jouin, Bretillot/Valette)
Pascale Cassagnau, Christophe Pillet

Roger Tallon
Chloé Braunstein, Gilles de Bure

Jasper Morrison
Charles-Arthur Boyer, Federica Zanco

Garouste et Bonetti
Pierre Staudenmeyer, Nadia Croquet, Laurent Le Bon

Borek Sipek
Philippe Louguet, Dagmar Sedlickà

Ron Arad
Raymond Guidot, Olivier Boissière

Andrea Branzi
François Burkhardt, Cristina Morozzi

NOÉ DUCHAUFOUR-LAWRANCE

DIRECTED BY EMMANUEL BERARD

AURÉLIEN FOUILLET

EMMANUEL BERARD

SUMMARY

For a Pluriversal Design

Like many other disciplines, design questions the transformations and crises that our societies undergo. Social, economic, and environmental transformations inspire a questioning of the practices and tools of design and the work of Noé Duchaufour-Lawrance is no exception, to the degree that its evolution allows us to perceive the impact of the elements that define our era.

Born in the 1970's, Noé Duchaufour-Lawrance is the fruition of a journey both eclectic and classical, perhaps more so than many of his contemporaries, and he seems to he seems to cultivate off beat paths, multiple experiences, explorations and challenges: he first studied sculpture, then design at the Paris School of Decorative Arts; he began his career by way of interior architecture, before dedicating himself to design… and we mustn't omit the surf culture that seems to have infused the life of this kite-surf practitioner and might even be the key to understanding his path.

Surfing through life

With a form that is oblong like a stretched egg and erect like an abstract totem, *Acqua*, a surfboard conceived for navigation and self-published in 2018, has a unique position amongst the hundreds of objects drawn by Noé Duchaufour-Lawrance. Its balanced, symmetrical formal purity responds to a decor that seems happenstance, beginning with a deep blue that outlines the rim, and then, as if by capillary action, washes over and atop the central surface. A surfboard? Of course. Watercolor? Without a doubt. But, *Acqua* is certainly and most of all a tool for this designer who seems to want to "surf through life"' carried along by the winds.

Noé Duchaufour-Lawrance's work is sensitive to its environment, cultivates a spontaneous, intuitive art, and is the expression of an era where the field of design attempts to explore a diversity of projects : to reintroduce beauty in industry, to unite the functionality and the utility of objects and to event attempt to propose eco-social forms in a context where politics, ecology and social advocacy increasingly intermingle. It's in this context where the question of the object navigates between modes of use value and exchange value ; from functioning as a direct link between humans and objects and as a symbolic mediation space been humans and objects ; from the beautiful and the useful, poles that we will explore in the work of Noé Duchaufour-Lawrance, in order to shed light on his theoretical positions and practices.

Aqua surfboard (2018) in Portugal.
Photo : Noé Duchaufour-Lawrance

Aristotle used the example of the sculptor to describe four types of causality active in the work of a visionary, an artist, a builder. Noé Duchaufour-Lawrance, who maintains a unique relationship with sculpture (both a familial legacy as well as an aspect of his initial training) reveals the traces of these four Aristotelian causes, and conceives his works by simultaneously exploring function, form, matter and competence.

Very in touch with our times, Noé Duchaufour-Lawrance is able to perceive the movements of water and air, as if the craft of a designer was a science that approaches meteorology, a sort of study of the climate of societies, a knowledge that decodes the sea spray of culture necessary for he who dares to throw himself in the waters to master the swell and carve an unprecedented path.

This path reveals itself through the conceptions of the object and of space that have characterized his work, a unique way of representing the world inspired by the emotions and sensations of nature – the natural world and vegetable world via new materials and new technologies — that allows us to perceive insight into our own era.

Master of the Universe

Noé Duchaufour-Lawrance achieved his early successes as an interior architect: an early creation was the London restaurant *Sketch* where we are projected into a space opera in which we discover the pod – toilettes that made his name, an experience that took the worlds of design and architectures by surprise. This was followed by *Senderens* where he worked with Majorelle's decor, and into which he succeeded in injecting a sustained contemporary dynamic that would be sustained from the *Yquem* dining room of the Hôtel Meurice, further on. The goldsmithing vocabulary of this tall native of Sauterne would combine with the well-rounded and balanced vocabulary of the Air France Business Lounge at the Charles de Gaulle Airport, in which we witness the unfolding dialogue between curves and vegetable forms… These projects, but a few amongst many more, are evidence of a unique vision of design and its stakes.

In his work, one can remark the influence of Art Nouveau, in particular a quest for harmonious alliance between materials and forms, where the organic, vegetable, natural dimensions are often brought to bear, or suggested. One can also perceive formal, graphic, or material vocabularies that recall the world of science fiction, as witnessed in the scenography of *Scènes d'intérieurs* at the the MAISON&OBJET salon in 2014, with its triangular, volcanic black forms, that remind one of the interstellar cruisers from *Star Wars.* They frame the expanses of water which itself expresses the more sensual relationship to be experienced in this scenography, connected calming elements in search of a

The *Sketch*'s bathroom, London (2000).
Photo : K. Hayden

harmony, an almost kinesthetic work of associated sounds, lights and materials.

This fictional dimension is encountered in the toilettes of *Sketch*, where the "eggs" and the lighting work together to present a space that is all at once organic, fantastic and intimate, and which projects us into a universe at the crossroads of the nostalgic kitsch of *Flash Gordon* and the subtle English spirit of Lewis Carroll's *Alice in Wonderland*. In even these few examples, each element composes a system of signs and objects that allow anyone who will to participate in the creation of meaning and the appropriation of the space thus created.

In an interview given to the Swiss newspaper, *Le Temps*, Noe Duchaufour-Lawrance shares a surprising reflection on the comparisons of the body and furniture, one and the other allowing us to communicate with our immediate spatial and temporal environment. Our philosophical tradition has clearly separated man from things, the spirit from the body, the subject and the object, the human being from the world around him, according to the expression consecrated by Descartes' "master and possessor of nature". It is thus, a priori, not part of our tradition to envisage the body and furniture as elements that determine our relationship to the world.

The ambition of design has, since its origins at the end of the 19th century, appeared to be to reintroduce sensuality where modern technique has made it disappear. Could there be something critical at work in this vision of design that interrogates its own arising in the very heart of modernity and industrial society?

There is, in any case, a desire in Noé Duchaufour-Lawrance to prioritize sensations and forms, to allow for the intervention of esthetics, in the etymological meaning, *aisthesis,* referring to sensation and beauty, through the display of a vision of objects, spaces and furniture that embody these notions. They aren't simple elements that certify the world in which we evolve. Just like in our own bodies, there is a link, an interface, or rather a network of relationships, both sensual and immaterial, that binds us to the world. This, in many ways, recalls what Baudrillard wrote, in order to demonstrate that before having an isolated utilitarian function, furniture has the immaterial function of containing our imagination·

The environments conceived by Noé Duchaufour-Lawrance suggest futurist worlds of James Bond films; or are organic: from the vegetable to the animal domains; or yet again, fantastic: from enchanted forests to bubbles suspended in space/time. All of this reflects his singular vision in which objects seem to describe a cosmos, form an order, a framework, a grammar of perception and meaning, and not a simple assembly of forms and materials.

The pod shaped toilets in *Sketch* seem like a foundational act in the work of Duchaufour-Lawrance, where the visitor is

The *Sketch*'s coatroom, London (2000).
Photo : K. Hayden

immersed in a cocoon for a sensory experience where curved forms, round forms of pink and white material engage in dialogue.

This cosmographic dimension in design is also encountered in the myth of an artisan of world : the demiurge. This Greek divinity who produced the cosmos (that which is ordered) out of chaos (that which is without form) bears a name which informs us a bit more about the unique cosmos that resonates in testimony from Noé Duchaufour-Lawrance: demiurge (*demos,* people and *ergon*, work) which we might translate as a conception of a collective form or collective work, a conception that invites us to perceive the communal, social dimension of design as a generator of relationships. This vision of design allows us to imagine a life of things with which we participate and which "fashions" our own, a life where the designer is a stage director and we, the actors.

For Duchaufour-Lawrance, objects speak to us and tell us stories, they carry meaning and narratives: hence, furniture and architecture are loaded with stories, memories, and shape an environment, which having become attractive, can develop a power of synchronicity. It is now capable of producing bonds between people, spaces, time, and things. A kind of shift of the useful to the beautiful, from the function of an object to its landscape. This is a vision where the object inscribes itself in an environment and takes on form, function and meaning, just as, inversely, it creates a space that it can

Manta desk (2006), edited by Ceccotti collezioni.
Photo: Riccardo Bianchi

integrate. The esthetic inhabits the useful, just as the useful resonates with the esthetic.

But this is just one aspect of the work of this designer who would never cease exploring other dimensions...

Art and Technique

Noé Duchaufour-Lawrance's works and methods create space for the articulation of a vocabulary. Representing nature is one of his recurrent leitmotivs but it isn't just a formal game. While the designer will find his inspiration therein, he will more than anything explores its limits. Perhaps the most important question of our era concerns the distinction between nature and artifice, between wildness and technique and it finds interesting resonances in his work.

If we take, for example, his *Manta* desk, or his most recent works, like the *Borghese* sofa, the *Mangrove* table or the *Roseau* vases, they all express a search for naturality. The sofa plays with vegetable motifs, stretching the curves and the branches, the umbrella pines of the Borghese villa provide the structure's vocabulary. The table explores the same register but with a different formal vocabulary, inversing the rhizome of the mangrove, in order to use it as a support. We won't dive into the mangrove; it will emerge of its own to support the surface. The *Manta* desk – one of his earliest works, which allowed him, for the first time, to formulate a particular "style" of his own – took inspiration in the lines revealed by the body of this aquatic bird, the Manta ray, purifying them and bringing them to a certain level of abstraction. The Manta ray's gills are also openings which give access to storage elements and echo both the aerian and aquatic curves of the desktop. *Manta* could be the desk of Jules Verne's Captain Nemo in his science fiction submarine, the Nautilus.

With influences from Art Nouveau – as already revealed through this esthetic vocabulary of naturally soft, fluidly structured forms, in service of a design and interior architecture conceived especially for the *Senderens* – Noé Duchaufour-Lawrance borrows a formal framework from nature, a style and an aesthetic, just as Gaudi in Spain, and Guimard in France did, to name the most famous of such predecessors. It's through this game and by way of style that forms become interesting for man, allowing him to appropriate them in an act of comprehension and creation. It's through works of art that nature allows itself to be seen. Objects create a landscape.

This naturalness, or rather its representation, this idealization of nature developed by Duchaufour-Lawrance, has nothing of the naivete of a primitivism or a return to some last paradise of nature.

In the work of Noé Duchaufour-Lawrance, the idea of naturality recalls his earliest images, this primitive phenomenology of affectivity, this association that we

Wall lamp from the *Naturoscopie* series (2012).

unconsciously construct between our affections, forms and materials. Here, nature is a resource of imagination, rich in forms, ideas, vocabularies and elements which constitute our symbolic and perceptive life. Thus, as a resource, nature can take on many very contemporary forms, materials and procedures, drifting far away from the natural as understood as a simple return to "bio-sourced" material or some kind "ecosomething" practice, which in general is little more than a pretext for marketing and greenwashing.

The composite materials, the digital technologies and forms combine and invite a questioning into the sensations of nature and their present occurrence. We rediscover this in his works like *Naturoscopie* The bookshelf, the lamps, and the console don't attempt to appear "natural", but rather evoke a sensation, a "natural" affection. Thus, the elements used are very contemporary, and the techniques, new. But this doesn't exclude the dynamics of evocation and convocation, quite the contrary. By way of a game of techniques and materials, nature is evoked through the angle of sensation rather than that of a flat image. And, if the sources of inspiration acknowledged here refer to cellular biology and astronomy, the interplay between macro and microcosmoses ultimately explodes into a form of technological poetry. In the *Naturoscopie* collection, an event occurs right where hologram and nature light meet, something that pierces through the canopy of the trees. There is an intensity of interplay between clarity and depth which expresses itself as an overlay of leaves and light, of movement and color. Here, technology and machinery are used to produce beauty and not simply the norms of repetition and uniformity. Although there's no direct filiation between Noé Duchaufour-Lawrance and the Bauhaus, one can't help but see in this perspective the realization of the ambitions expressed by the movement's founder, Walter Gropius, when he called on creators to take up new technologies of fabrication in order to imagine new forms of beauty: "It's from the particularity of the Machine that the new beauty of its products is born." Noé Duchaufour-Lawrance is part of a deep current of creators exploring the possibilities of technology, in order to push the limits and find new categories of beauty.

We encounter this dialogue again though another point of view in his work as a designer. Here are contemporary modern, lively forms, which are associated with raw materials and traditional knowledge. Thus, in his series of rugs, *Raw*, he explores our origins, presenting a form of raw stone that evokes the initial human arts, flint and two sided stone tools, all the while playing on the monumental presence of the pieces that he presents like megaliths in the storefront windows of their editor. And again, in *Eros 433*, he confronts the form and brutality of black lava stone, which can't help but recall the monolith in *2001: A Space Odyssey*, and our ever-ambiguous relationship to the object and to techniques.

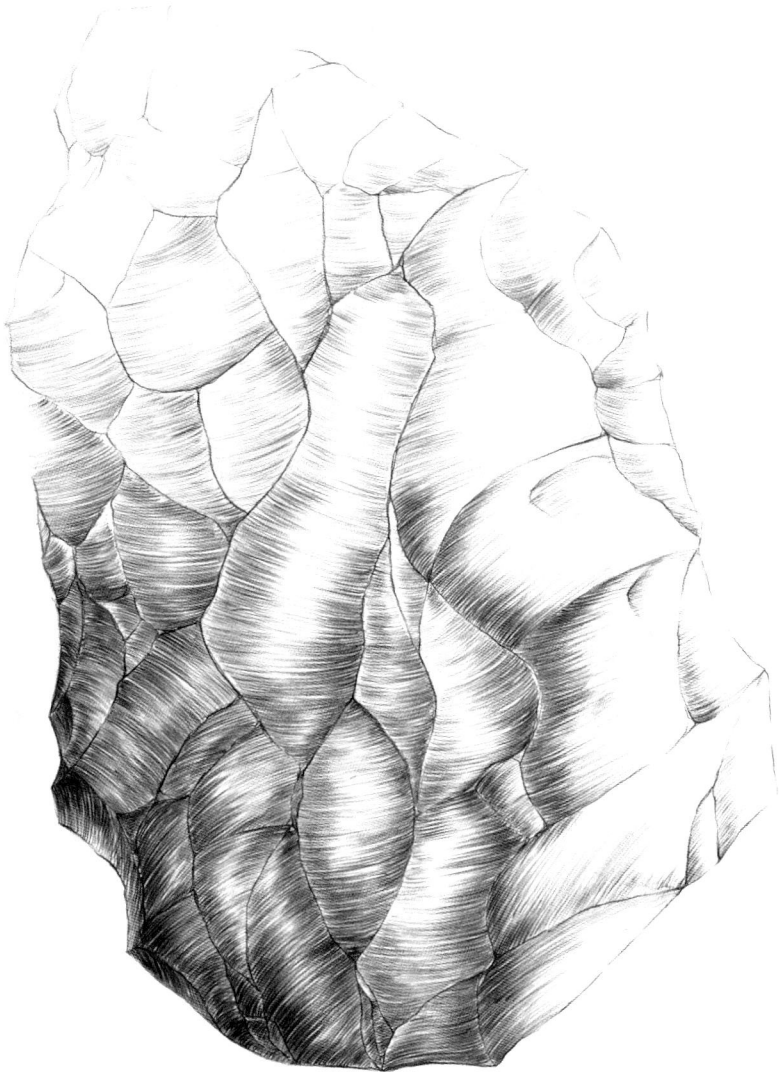

Drawing for the *Raw* carpet collection (2019) édited by Tai Ping.

It's a relationship which we see evolving over the last decades from a language of expertise to one of magic. If the object of the 20th century, when it is technical, shows complexity, strength and technicity, the object of this beginning of the 21st century accomplishes the promise of a technology that tends to disappear, because it hides itself, veils itself. Thus, our smartphones are testimony of a cutting-edge technology that present themselves as little magic monoliths. We also find this in *Landscape*, where the quasi spatial form marries the craftsmanship of Longchamp with the imaginary landscape of sand and forms that recalls the science fiction world of Fran Herbert's *Dune*, seen through cinema vision of David Lynch. Let us also not forget the pieces found in the *Transmissions* collection, where the shell is made of natural materials (linen and white leather) that give the sensation of an artificial skin. Here, the craftsmanship allows the material to arise and reveal, if still necessary, that the history of craftwork, at least that of the avant-garde, is one of innovation·

This combination of the natural and the artificial is a relationship that our era and our societies redefine, powerfully. It's a combination that isn't necessarily neutral and which explores the frontiers between nature and culture.

What relationship do we maintain with "nature" in a world where the artifacts of industry have even invaded the depths of the oceans? Is not our environment one of cities

Transmission collection (2016)
designed at the Mobilier national's atelier de recherche et de création.
Photo: Thibaud Chapotot

that have become "machines for living", since now over 50%
of the world's population inhabit them? There is the feeling
of an almost inherent tension of living between these two
elements of the natural and the technical. These are
combinations and questions about them are at the heart of
Duchaufour-Lawrance's evolving vision.

Wouldn't it be nice?

Thus, the combination of the archaic and technological,
born of the industrial revolution and the emergence of
consumer society, has not only produced the masterpieces of
architecture, art and design, but has also profoundly
transformed our relationship to the world.

Some see in this commercial, industrial, mercantile and
even serial aspect a characteristic element of design. The
stage described *MAYA* (Most Advanced Yet Acceptable), by
Raymond Loewy is perhaps the best illustration: if the
designer must innovate, invent, and create, he should never
directly undermine the consumer's current convictions.

Others, on the contrary, see design as a movement of
resistance, or at the very least, an element capable of
correcting some of the more perverse effects of the
industrialization and consumerization, which is the case of
William Morris or of Andrea Branzi who wrote in *Il design*

italiano: "Embellishing reality should no longer be considered an act of diversion or submission, but rather an integral act in the project of the transformation of the world."

The work of Noé Duchaufour-Lawrance questions this industry of beauty that is design: if William Morris wishes to reintroduce beauty in industry, should we conclude that industry has contaminated beauty? Isn't the increased formatting of the world an evident symptom of this process?

The deeper meaning of these questions about the possible relationship between beauty and industry, between man and technique can be found in Noé Duchaufour-Lawrance's powerful piece, *Marée noire au clair de lune (Black Tide in the Moonlight)*. In this ensemble, he rearranges the codes and values of beauty. It is an essentially black room that vibrates with a reflective light. It is both creamy and mysterious and allows us to recall this material that threatens to destroy the plant in Luc Besson's film, *The Fifth Element*. Does it reflect a deeply personal question or a lucid perception of the stakes of our era? In any event, we detect therein this ambiguity of a beauty that manifests itself in destruction, also evoked by the title of this work.

Far from the modern ideal that associates human progress with the mastery of savage nature, Noé Duchaufour-Lawrance brings a lucid gaze on the practices and challenges

Marée noire au clair de lune collection (2009), galerie Pierre Bergé, Brussels.

of design in their industrial dimension, of course, but also to modes of conception, modes of relationship in both fabrication and distribution. This gaze uncovers a troubling beauty in the industrial world, and allows the fleeting perception of the iridescences of a sheet of oil spill provoked by its reflection under moonlight.

Is this his invitation for us to see the beauty of the industrial world? Or does he simply encourage a more critical reflection on this world, in order to imagine the models of tomorrow? The unfoldment of his journey seems to encourage us in the latter direction…

Design for the pluriverse

As though in response to *Marée noire au clair de lune*, there is in the current work of this designer a kind of "correspondence", to borrow the Baudlerian theme, between objects and the world. This idea is developed in his work by a kind of return to the source, to craftsmanship, to raw material and to territory. This is what he explores, for example, in the *Caractère* collection, in which we witness a dialogue between material and drawing. The material is raw, intuitive.

He is also committed to research into the possibility of working "beyond constraint", and over long periods of exploration, exchange, conception and fabrication. This is what he is currently developing in Portugal with the project called, *Made in Situ*. It's an anchoring by way of a tool and the material discovered through the course of voyages, into the context of fabrication, conception, and craftsmanship that create the constellation that is a culture, and testify to a will to encourage the encounter between objects, humans, and territoriality.

Following through in continuity with *Caractère*, Noé Duchaufour-Lawrance again questions design practices through an approach that one could qualify as "territorial", contextualizing conception and production in echo with the precepts of the "Slow" movement. Re - localizing, giving time to time, connecting with local material and culture, are all ways to that inhabit his work. Giving value to «manual labor», to artisan craftsmanship, such that he develops a design where man is at the heart of things. "Asking real questions about manual work", writes Crawford, "means asking real questions about the nature of human life. To understand what it means to be human, one must understand the manual interaction between man and the world."

Excellence in craftsmanship, a capacity to innovate and create, as well as a sense of its own history are, for Noé Duchaufour-Lawrance, ingredients of a "nouveau" design. It's a dynamic in which he rediscovers the fundamentals of being a "sculptor-designer", a *man of many turns*, surfing and exploring all the diversity available to nourish him and create amidst the multiplicity.

Caractère dinnerware collection (2018), édited par Revol.
Photo: Sanda Vuckovic

In this, he goes against the current of a history of art and design that has separated the artist from the artisan, the visionary from the craftsman. It's an old quarrel that goes back to the creation of the Academies of drawing, out of a need for freedom from the medieval corporations. He is also against the current of the idea developed by Vasari in his "Lives of the Artists", according to which a work is solely the product of the interior life of the creator. Noé Duchaufour-Lawrance prefers to reconnect with a hybrid being which is, amongst other things, connected to a contemporary dynamic, witnessing increasing ambiguity at the frontiers of the arts, design and craftsmanship. Frontiers that define the beautiful, the good, progress, and design are today under great criticism, open to challenge, allowing the competencies of the crafts that incarnate them to mix and restructure themselves. Most certainly, Noé Duchaufour-Lawrance is a polymorphic designer, metamorphic, given to multiple facets and tastes. He has a precise humanistic vision of the fabrication of objects that echoes the idea developed by Gilbert Simondon: "The crafty man is the one that the world accepts."

Crafting a link between territory and the object, between the craftsman and the visionary participates in the redefinition of the perimeter of the creation of a designer and the ecosystem, the heartland in which that creation takes root.

(up) Caramulo rocks, Portugal (2020).
Photo: Noé Duchaufour Lawrance

(down) *Caramulo* lamps (2020), from the first "Made in Situ" collection.
Photo : Sanda Pagaimo

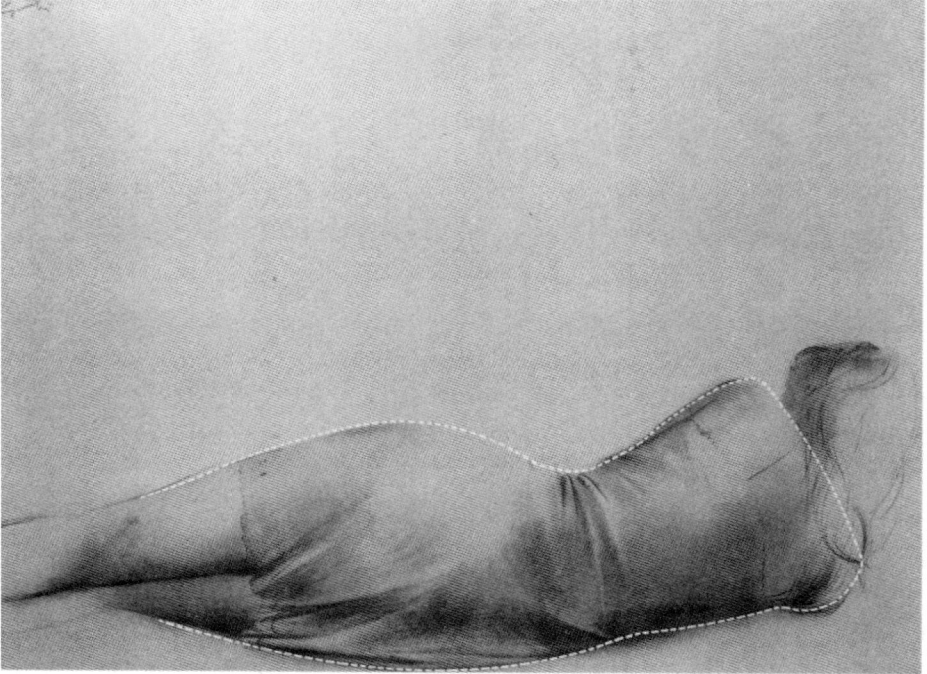

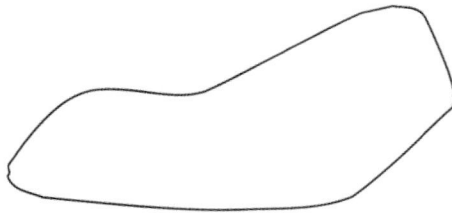

Schéma d'un plateau de table en verre inspiré
d'un dessin de Léonor Fini.

Excerpt from "L'étrange univers de l'architecte Carlo Molino" catalog,
published by Centre Pompidou, Paris, 1989.

Without doubt, this is the kind of resonance in work that brought Bruno Taut and then Charlotte Perriand to Japan, and whose vocation is to honor ancestral and vernacular knowledge that populates and animates Japanese culture.

Several "periods" punctuate Noé Duchaufour-Lawrance's body of work. From Pierre Paulin to Charlotte Perriand, from Art Nouveau to Bauhaus, from industrial to humanist design, so many influences and points of view that illuminate his trajectory.

Fundamentally an adept of a total art in service of design, and from there an observer and revealer of the work of nature, he seems, today, to incline towards a transmission of objects bearing meaning and memory, sign objects, almost mythological, and territories with multiple access points, where material encounters human craftsmanship.

All of these are the elements of a creator who is a reflection of his era and its challenges. There is a bit of the Beach Boys, a bit of James Bond, a bit of Kubrick, and as a polymorphic navigator, Noé Duchaufour-Lawrance upsets the codes of his discipline, of all disciples. He said, in regards to Carlo Mollino: "It's his philosophy that I find fabulous, his multidisciplinary side. He was at the same time architect, designer and poet…" One must believe that his principal project is to open and perpetually stretch his field of creation, by placing man at the heart of design. It's a vision that is dominated neither by hegemony nor the universalism of a particular culture, but rather an adaptive multiplicity for a design that is pluriversal.

Notes

[1] Joël de Rosnay, *Surfing Through Life*, 2012.

[2] Ludovic Duhem (dir), *Ecosocial Design*, 2018.

[3] Karl Marx, *Capital, I*, 1867: "The usefulness of a thing makes its use value." & "Exchange-value appears, first of all, as *quantitative relationship,* the proportion in which use - values of one kind are exchanged for use - values of another kind."

[4] The efficient cause; the formal cause, the material cause and the final cause.

[5] *Sketch*, Club-Restaurant, London, 2002.

[6] *Senderens*, Restaurant, Paris, 2005.

[7] *Yquem*, Le Meurice, Dining Room, Paris, 2012.

[8] *Air France Business Lounge*, Roissy Airport S4, Paris, 2012.

[9] Interview with Isabelle Cerboneschi, 2016 "Furniture is what comes closest to the body after clothing, but I find it interesting to create a connection both with the corporeal and the emotional. I love when people caress objects. The most beautiful compliment that someone can make about my furniture is when someone caresses it. This generates an attachment, which allows me to create a patina. For me, a piece of furniture is well lived when it possesses this patina that shows that it has been loved."

[10] René Descartes, *Discourse on Method*, 1637.

[11] They seem rather like tools, elements by which man dominates by impressing his vision and his form. Here, science and technique are also conceived as elements of power. The engineer or the erudite are both inheritors and representatives.

[12] Let us remember the often violent indictments of John Ruskin (John Ruskin, *The Nature of the Gothic*, 1854) concerning industry and printing, in which he denounced the resulting uniformization: "I hear the quaking of the printing press… and the cannon powder – the two great plagues of our era – and I begin to say to myself that the abominable art of the printing press is the root of all ills: it will encourage people to treat all things the same way.

[13] Jean Baudrillard, *The system of objects*, 1968.

[14] Platon, *Timée*.

[15] Let us recall that the Greek word Kósmos refers to good order but also to ornament.

[16] Carl Gustav Jung, *Paracelsica*, 2001: synchronicity is a link in meaning.

[17] *Manta* Desk, Ceccotti Collezioni, 2006.

[18] *Borghese* Couch, La Chance, 2018.

[19] *Mangrove* Table, NDL Editions, 2015.

[20] Vase *Roseau*, Ligne Roset, 2009.

[21] As Alain Roger demonstrated: there is an artificialization of things, and nature isn't artistic by itself, it becomes so in contact with us. It is for us to find in it forms that were up to now unknown by it.

[22] Gaston Bachelard, *The Poetics of Space*, 1957.

[23] *Naturoscopie* Collection, Galerie BS, 2012.

[24] Walter Gropius, *Buildings and Projects*, 1995.

[25] *Raw* Collection, Tai Ping, 2019.

[26] Guéridon *Eros 433*, NDL Editions, 2017.

[27] Desk Ensemble *Landscape*, Longchamp, 2008.

[28] *Transmissions* Collection, Workshop for research and Creation, Mobilier National, 2016.

[29] If, like Alain writes in *System of the Fine Arts*: "The engineer transforms the dexterity of the artisan into that of a machine.", it would seem here that the artisan and the designer, in their cooperation, transform the gesture of the machine into a poetic creation, where the artisanal gesture is taken to new heights of perfection through technology.

[30] Isn't it our very human nature, by the way, to produce the artificial, as Hannah Arendt suggested in *The Condition of Modern Man*, 1961: "Men constantly create fabricated conditions that are their own, in spite of their background or varying beauty, and all have the same conditioning force upon natural objects"?

[31] Alexandra Midal in *La Manufacture du meurtre*, 2018, reveals to us, with a certain amusement, the link between the industrial revolution and the figure of the serial killer. Far from being a coincidence this prophesizes new approaches to production of which the assembly line and the serial killer are just two expressions.

[32] Raymond Loewy, *Ugliness Sells Badly*, 1953.

13 Or, as was written by Abraham Moles in *Psychology of kitsch:* "The designer doesn't claim to be a "great artist", not because the supermarket can't afford it, but because the great artists is ahead of his time, only followed by a micro milieu, and the masses are far behind him, whereas the designer is positioned axiomatically at the level of optimum psychological acceptance."

34 Let us recall the warnings of Adorno and Horkheimer (*The Dialectic of Enlightenment, 1944*) concerning industrial society: " The fact that the ascepticized factory and everything that is a part of it brutally liquidates the metaphysic could be indifferent, but if it itself becomes a metaphysic, an ideological curtain behind which is concentrated the disaster of the real, then it is not at all indifferent." The fact that industry caused ancient metaphysics to tumble isn't a problem as such, but attention should be paid that it not in its turn become one in its place, and that everything that makes us human be not erased by the machine. Or to recall the wise words of Günther Anders (Gunther Anders, *The Outdatedness of Human Being*, 1956), let us be careful that the self-made man doesn't go from being a man who creates into a man who builds, repairs and replaces, as is the case with contemporary consumer society.

35 *Black Tide in the Moonlight*, Galerie Pierre Bergé, Bruxelles, 2008.

36 *Caractère*, Revol, 2018.

37 The idea according to which one should slow down the rhythms of life, production, consumption, etc.

38 Mathew B. Crawford, *Shop Class as Soulcraft: An Inquiry Into the Value of Work,* 2009.

39 To repeat here the mythical figure, one of Ulysses, a navigator and artisan designer of the Trojan Horse.

40 Gilbert Simondon, *On the Mode of Existence of Technical Objects*, 1958.

41 In Noé Duchaufour-Lawrance: "Furniture is what is closest to us, besides clothing" interview with Marion Vignal, Coté Maison, 2012.

42 Arturo Escobar, *Design for the pluriverse*, 2018.4

Bertrand Bougé,
Noé Duchaufour-Lawrance's father.

My Other Land by the Sea

*A*n awful lot of who I am today is related to my parents; they have made me who I am and what I do today is connected to this history and to my childhood memories.

My father, the eldest of three sons from a family of Lorraine shopkeepers, went to Paris to do his studies at the prestigious Polytechnique school. He soon realized that these studies did not really correspond to what he wanted to do and be, so he followed in parallel evening classes at the school of Beaux-Arts, learnt to draw, to engrave and he finally decided to devote himself to sculpture. With the money his father offered him to celebrate his graduation from Polytechnique and to buy himself a smart car, he bought an old Citroën 2CV and a set of sculptor's tools and began a "tour de France" during which he visited sculptors with whom he perfected his sculptural skills. A car breakdown stopped him in the Aveyron department, in Saint Laurent d'Olt, where he bought a house

Primel Tregastel shore in Plougasnou, Brittany.
Photo: Noé Duchaufour-Lawrance

and settled in with my mother, whom he had met some months earlier in Bonneval sur Arc. My mother had studied at the School of Beaux-Arts in Nancy, and was working in a pancake house in this village in the Alps. I was born in Mende, and spent some of my first year in this very rustic house, without electricity or running water. My father was often absent, continuing his journey of discovery on the roads of the region and beyond, and I think that deep down, he was not ready for this new family, right away. My mother then decided to take me to Paris and to separate from my father who was completely engrossed in his research. He died six months later. With my mother we stayed in Paris until I was 6. My mother gave art classes and we lived near the Parc Monceau, a smart neighborhood, in an apartment loaned by my mother's friends. We spent our holidays in the house in Aveyron where I felt the absence of this father who I learnt was a sculptor. My mother then met the man who was to become my adoptive father and we left Paris to settle in Brittany, in North Finistère. This is where I discovered nature, the sea, the wind, stone... during long walks that were more or less the only thing to do... It was only when I was 13 that my mother told me the reasons of my father's death: exhausted, in conflict with his family and their expectations of him, he had taken his own life. I took this gesture as being a sort of message, a passing of the baton, and I decided, in turn, to go for an artistic career…

... and you became a designer...

Yes, because the life of an artist was a source of fear for me, maybe fear of falling into a void where I was going to have to confront myself... Having to apply creation to something, to find a function for it was more reassuring for me. But down in Brittany I did not really have much opportunity to form an idea of what design could be apart from the discovery of some pieces by Philippe Starck in French mail-order catalogues and my uncle's collection of Art Nouveau objects. We went to visit this uncle, a pharmacist, once a year in Paris and it was at his home that I saw a few pieces of Bugatti[1] furniture, and some glass objects by Gallé or Daum... So armed with this smattering of artistic culture, I did a course leading to a F12 Baccalauréat (Arts applied to industry) in Brest. During summer breaks I had work placements with Yann Kersalé and Arval, an architectural agency set up by friends of my father[2]. These experiences familiarized me with the world of architecture. Then, my adoptive father, who is English and who never wanted to interfere or intervene in my desires but who always accompanied them with great sensitivity, gave me an article from a magazine he had brought back from London on Ron

[1] Carlo Bugatti (1856 -1940), Italian cabinetmaker and decorator trained in France where he settled and obtained his first successes at the start of the 20th century. His style blends art nouveau with oriental influences.
[2] Yann Kersalé (born 1955) is a French artist whose work with light installations combines architecture and landscaping. Co-founders of the architectural agency ARVAL, Bertrand Mathieu and Alain-Marc Piel are architects and urbanists.

Sculptor Philolaos and his daughter, Isabelle Tloupas, in his workshop (circa 1978).

Terrace in Rabat, Morocco (1996).
Photo : Noé Duchaufour-Lawrance

Arad. In this article I discovered this incredible work, hi-fi systems made of concrete, welded metal furniture... and I understood that one can be both a sculptor and a designer! This was the trigger that led me to enrol in the Paris school Olivier de Serres[3] , in the metal sculpture section. At that time I often saw good friends of my mother, the sculptor Philolaos[4] and his wife Marina Assaël. With my mother we spent time with them and I was able to observe Philolaos at work, in a very disciplined way, every day in his workshop. There was for me a kind of obligation to learn sculpture and, in so doing to bind myself to my absent father, because I was convinced that he had tried to transmit this to me. I only did two years at Olivier de Serres because of the sense of frustration I had with the absence of function in the pieces I was making. I therefore joined the third year of the Paris School of Decorative Arts[5]. It was a big change for me, and quite difficult because I was coming from a course where I was making things in a hands-on sort of way, and in the 'Arts Déco' the work seemed more theoretical. In my first year there I soon made a beeline for the workshops.

[3] The National School of Applied Arts and Crafts (Ensaama), located in Paris, rue Olivier de Serres.
[4] Philolaos Tloupas (1923 - 2010) Greek sculptor who settled in France in 1950. Faithful to his craft heritage, his work in stainless steel combines realism and minimalism. He also designed furniture and utility objects.
[5] École Nationale Supérieure des Arts Décoratifs (ENSAD), Paris.

I was a little confused at the end of that year and I negotiated a gap year. It was spent in Morocco, where my partner of the time was teaching theater, in Rabat. I spent my days in a small cabin by the sea tinkering, drawing... I also spent some of my time in the workshop of a Moroccan cabinet maker and sculptor, Jamil Bennani, and it was there that I met Jonathan Amar[6] who was involved in interior decoration for villas and restaurants in Morocco and in France. As he saw that I could draw, he asked me to draw perspectives for his projects and thus it was that I started to work, in dilettante mode.

Back in Paris, at the Arts Déco for my 4th and final year, I was about to become a father. It was during this year that I designed and created the *Manta* desk, in white lacquered carbon fiber. So I moved from metal sculpture, very rough, quite expressive, to a desk executed in a composite material, very light and with a sophisticated silhouette. This change took place during my final year at the School, which had changed during my absence and where I met people who are, even today, my friends. The class was greatly influenced by one of the students, a former "compagnon" (member of a

[6] A Franco-moroccan interior designer, Jonathan Amar was responsible, in the 1980's, for the décor of a number of Parisian venues tincluding the *Joe Allen*, at les Halles. His eclectic style which mixed cultures was much sought after on both sides of the Mediterranean. In 1985, he became artistic director at the *Bains-Douches*, went on to relook the *Piscine Deligny*, and, in 1990, to give the *Palace* discotheque a new lease of life. Today he is a designer.

craftsmen's guild) who created a group dynamic different from what I had known before leaving for Morocco.

I had the great fortune of having as my design teacher Jean-Claude Maugirard[7], with whom I exchanged a lot and who helped, accompanied and encouraged me in my approach which was then more the approach of a plastic artist, and not quite what the school expected of me. Jean-Claude's courses were in fact great discussions to which he brought his references and his culture. He knew how to explore everyone's potential and let it flourish. He never tried to shackle me to orthodox design, but on the contrary, he let me develop my ideas. Whereas some of my fellow students chose the subject of their diploma according to the personalities of the members of the jury in order to impress them and, perhaps later, to be edited by them, I was in a somewhat different register and I proposed this desk, half-way between sculpture and design.

So the Manta *desk was your first piece of furniture?*

Not quite, before the *Manta* desk, there was another piece, a large table, which was more like a trampoline than a table…

---

[7] Born in 1940, Jean-Claude Maugirard studied at the Ecole Boule in Paris. As a designer, he taught at the Ensad at the same time as writing and organizing exhibitions. En 1979, he founded, at the behest of the French ministry of industry, the VIA (valorisation de l'innovation dans l'ameublement) and remained director of this important promoter of design until 1994.

Manta desk facing the sea.
Photo: Jérome Tarby

the top (three meters long!) was composed of canvas
stretched by a very complex, very technical system. It was my
first object, conceived in my first year at Arts Déco, when I
shut myself away in the workshop of Christian Borger,
responsible for the metal workshop.

It was so large that, as I was not able to store it at home
during my stay in Morocco, it was stored in the hall of the
school, during this year! To return to the Manta desk, I came
back from Morocco where I had spent a very, let's say, restful
year... It was my last year at ENSAD and I was starting to try
to understand the environment I found myself in, the world
of Design. At that time, I was very interested in the work of
an editor, Cappelini[8], then in full growth and who commercialized pieces demonstrating an appetite for a certain modernity
implementing the latest technologies. I was seduced by this
new liberty and the smooth, futuristic forms of, for example,
the *Statuette* chair of Lloyd Schwan[9]. It was also this
vocabulary that inspired me for the *Manta* desk. To realize it I
worked with a designer of aircraft interiors, Catherineau, in
the Bordeaux region to whom I brought the model of the
piece I wanted to make. It was really a science fiction desk
with a bit of James Bond. At the same time, I wanted it to be
light and airy. So I was accepted for a month and a half in this

[8] A family business set up after the war, Cappelini made a name for itself from the 1970's
onwards with the commercialization of ambitious furniture designed by Shiro Kuramata,
Alessandro Mendini…
[9] *Statuette* chair by Lloyd Schwan edited by Cappelini in 1995.

company to work flat out on my project, assisted by two technicians on contract (whose names I have unfortunately forgotten). The company let us use all its scraps of materials (carbon fiber, kevlar…) and its molds. It was from this assembly of precious materials that this desk was made. It was then painted in a pearly white which had iridescent reflections… we were approaching an aesthetic of "tuning" but it corresponded to what I had in mind, a real presence and at the same time almost invisible, evanescent. This desk, which was above all a sort of test, was also a piece of pure expression. In addition, it came from a wooden model and not from a drawing. At that time, I took an infinite amount of time, and a lot of pleasure too, in making these models: the structure was in layered balsa wood. Then everything was painted. That's about all I produced that year: this desk and a baby!

The desk was not very well received on the day of the jury… I remember in particular the somewhat scathing reflection of Chantal Hamaide[10] who wondered aloud in front of the other members of the jury if this object was not rather intended to seduce them than to serve as a desk! I was left dumbstruck, without arguments… I had really put all my guts into this project.

[10] Chantal Hamaide, journalist, exhibition curator, founder in 1985 of "Intramuros", the first magazine dedicated solely to Design. She was its editor in chief until 2017. Open to new trends and encouraging of new talents, she nevertheless defended a somewhat orthodox vision of industrial design.

In the end, I still obtained the validation of the jury and this desk ended up at my home, suspended from the ceiling of the garage of a small house that I occupied in Montreuil. Some time later, Jean-Claude Maugirard put pressure on the VIA for the desk to be presented in an exhibition of works by former students of the School. Again, I encountered a lot of resistance, especially from the director of VIA who did not recognize the work of a designer in this desk but rather that of a sculptor.

Ah! Quite a promising start ...

Absolutely! In fact, it was in complete opposition to the idea that people had of design at the time. That said, I went back to work in my workshop, in Montreuil, to make a new model of this desk. It wasn't until a few years later, in 2000, that I discovered the Italian editor Ceccotti Collezioni at the Milan Furniture Fair. That year, I saw an incredible chair by Ross Lovegrove, the *Bone Chair,* completely organic, in wood and carbon[11]. A piece of pure sculpture! It was the trigger that encouraged me to imagine a wooden version of the *Manta* desk in order to propose it to Cecotti. I made new models and above all, I designed a total environment in which I installed the desk. At that time I had with me a collaborator, Sébastien

[11] *Bone Chair* by Ross Lovegrove commercialized by Ceccotti Collezioni in 1994.

Kieffer, who was to work with me in the following 8 years. Sébastien was an expert in 3D and we had great fun together navigating around this universe, traveling between the curves of this desk, visiting all its details which seemed like architectures to us… It was wonderful to be able to get lost, like that, in the scale of the object. And it was this project, this complete universe with, in the center, the desk, that I proposed to Cecotti the following year. I went up to their stand at the Milan Furniture Fair, with my folder of drawings under my arm and asked them if they could take a look at my project. At first they politely explained that it was not the right time or place, but I insisted… At that moment Franco Ceccotti arrived with Roberto Lazzeroni, who was at the time artistic director of Ceccotti Collezioni, they looked at my project, the drawings… I do not understand Italian well but they spoke a lot among themselves and at one point, I understood that they were saying it would be for Milan, the following year! I was incredibly happy. Happy because it was a piece into which I had put a lot of myself. It was not my first collaboration with an editor because a few years earlier I had been lucky enough to meet Eleonora and Francesca Zanotta, who had accepted to commercialize the table and console *Dessous chics*[12], pieces more in tune with the times but which

[12] Released in 2005 by the Italian editor Zanotta, the series of tables and consoles *Dessous chics* plays with the codes of the 18th century French Rocaille style to leave just the silhouette visible between the legs.

didn't suit me that well. Following that, we worked together on projects which suited me better and which I found more coherent. Ceccotti's *Manta* collection took three years to develop and finally came out in 2006. Ceccotti were quite used to making complex pieces but they realized that it was a much more "crazy" project, more dreamlike than those which constituted their catalogue. From the start, given the complexity of its manufacture and the time required for the teams to make it, they decided to produce just 20 copies. Right from its first presentation, the desk was a great success and the first twenty pieces were sold quickly. But this adventure was above all the beginning of a long collaboration and of a great friendship.

...Let's go back to 1996. You've just become a father, you've graduated from the ENSAD with the Manta *desk, and you've settled in Paris. And then ?*

A few years earlier, a friend had put me in contact with a modeling agency and I took part in photo shoots of advertising campaigns for consumer brands. It worked quite well and it allowed me to finance my creative projects as well as to support my family. This activity was very useful but I did not take it too seriously. I traveled a lot (I discovered Japan thanks to these photo shoots). At the same time I worked in collaboration with the scenographer Clémence Farrell and the set designer Christophe Labbé[13] , with whom I drew roughs of sets for advertising films, and even movie props and costumes[14].

And then came your first interior design project the Sketch[15], *in London*

Indeed, in Paris I once again crossed the path of Jonathan Amar whom I had met in Morocco a few years earlier. He told me about a project he was working on for his friend, Mourad Mazouz[16], in London. Jonathan was then very busy in Paris: cafes, restaurants and nightclubs, and asked if I could help him with this « remote » project. I had a lot of freedom to imagine the decor and I started drawing, a lot, day and night. Jonathan would end up abandoning this very complicated project, leaving me the freedom to pursue it with Mourad. From this project come the "eggs" which still house the toilets of this restaurant and which have been seen all around the world. Other designers were also invited, along the way, to

[13] Met while at the Ensad, Christophe Labbé is a set designer for advertising campaigns and the cinema. Clémence Farrell, another graduate of the Ensad, is a scenographer and designer.
[14] For example for the film by Cédric Klapisch, *Peut-être*, released in November 1999
[15] In a protected building in Mayfair, London, the *Sketch*, is a restaurant-club which opened in December 2002. Thanks to its interiors - 2500 square mètres on several levels - and its menu - signed by Pierre Gagnaire - it soon became a fashionable venue.
[16] Mourad Mazouz (born in 1962) opened his first Paris restaurant in 1988, the *Bascou* followed by the opening of the *404*. His Parisian successes encouraged him to embark on the conquest of London with the opening of a couscous restaurant *Momo*'s in 1997.

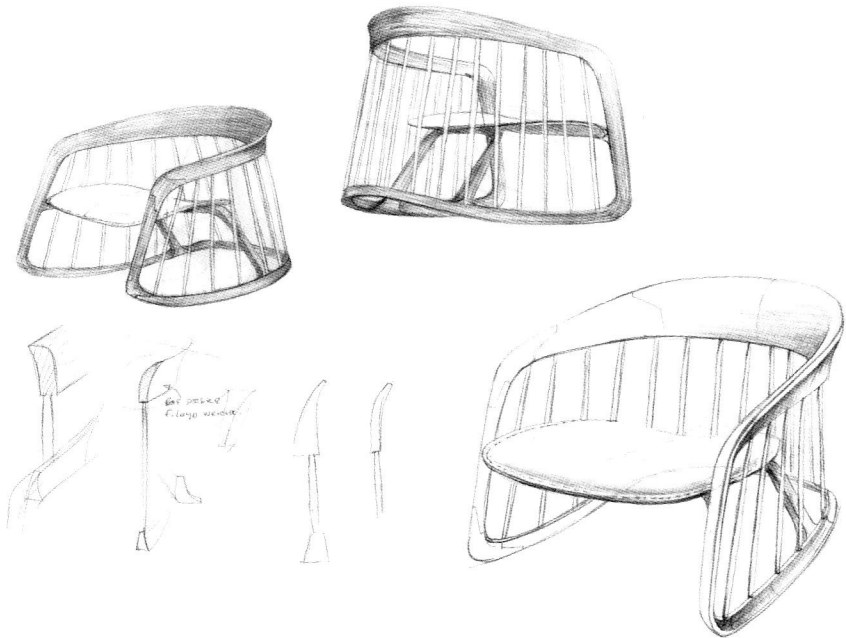

Drawings for the *Harper* rocking-chair, edited by par Bernhardt design (2014).

join this adventure: it was on this project, at a time when I was fresh out of school, that I met Ron Arad and Marc Newson who also contributed to the interiors of the *Sketch*. The project finished way behind schedule, went through innumerable ups and downs and, in all, lasted four years, four years of intense work and stress. I came out of it exhausted, a little worn down and without really getting the recognition that I hoped for. In this register, the promoter of this project, Mourad Mazouz, and Newson and Arad were much better at putting themselves in the spotlight than me, a young unknown of 28. After this project, I was ready to chuck it all in and go to live another life. I remember Mourad saying that if the Sketch didn't work out, he would be happy selling ice creams on the beach in Ibiza. For my part I was ready to raise goats on the Larzac plateau! But I was retained by another project, the competition for the redevelopment of the *Senderens* Restaurant in Paris[17]. I was invited to compete by Nelly Rodi[18] who pressed Alain Senderens to organize this consultation. I was chosen, but I was given a very tight budget and just three and a half months to deliver everything. I still do not understand by what miracle we managed to complete this project on time. These two projects were really a sort of launch pad for me.

[17] Previously the *Lucas Carton*, place de la Madeleine, the *Senderens* reopened in 2005 under its new chef, Alain Senderens.
[18] Nelly-Claire Rodi created the agency NellyRodi in 1985 . It soon became an influential trend-setting agecy, advising many ready-to-wear, decoration and lifestyle companies. The agency is now run by her son, Pierre-François Le Louët.

But they still couldn't be considered pure design...?

In fact, I had a lot of difficulty separating an object from its physical environment. The two were inseparable for me and in my projects I tried to design a particular environment for each piece of furniture or object. Fortunately, I don't have that hang up today, but at the time, each object had to have an associated space, even a fantasy. It was this idea that I implemented both in the *Sketch* (in the famous staircase of the "eggs" it is these objects that draw the architecture of the space) and in *Senderens* where I had drawn each piece of furniture and each *Cocoon* light fitting on the ceiling as an extension of the existing carved wood structures of Majorelle[19]. My approach was undoubtedly influenced by Art Nouveau or the work of Pierre Paulin in which furniture is architecture and vice versa. At that time I also had another passion: I must have seen *2001, Space Odyssey* dozens of times and I was very marked by this incredible and total aesthetic universe.

You told us earlier that Manta *had been conceived in volume, rather than in drawings... what is your relation to drawing ?*

When I look at my early furniture designs today, I find them rather awkward... I expressed myself much better in

[19] In 1880 the new owner, M. Scaliet placed an order for wooden decorations with the craftsman Louis Majorelle (1859 - 1926), a rising star of 'art nouveau. These decorations helped make the *Lucas* a restaurant dear to the hearts of art lovers and are protected as a national heritage.

volume and therefore I made models in order to communicate my ideas more precisely. It took me some time to
improve my drawing and it was thanks to a self-discipline, to
a framework that I imposed on myself that I managed to draw
with enough precision to be understood. Michel Roset[20], with
whom I leafed through my sketchbooks a lot, said to me one
day « you should just let the pencil flow a bit more ». And he
was right, I had to step back, because I was losing sight of the
object's function. I realized that I was entering a comfort zone
which could jeopardize my creative desires. So I tried to
change my way of working.

Little by little, I moved away from this rigorous designer
work on form and I left, in my drawing, some room for a
slightly freer expression, in which chance, imperfection,
sometimes even awkwardness have their place, and in which
the dialogue between the teams of the manufacturer or the
editor, can have an effect on the final form.

When I was searching for ideas for the collection of rugs
for Tai Ping[21], I drew minerals. I gave Tai Ping a series of
drawings and they did a wonderful job of translating the
drawings into textures and volumes... The textile palette, with

[20] Michel Roset (born 1949) inherited his family's business (manufacture of upholstered furniture dating from the 1930's) and extended this business in 1975 with the Cinna brand, which had a more innovative approach to contemporary furniture. Cinna has commercialized several pieces by Noé Duchaufour-Lawrance, including the *Ottoman* series (2010).
[21] Inspired by the tectonic force of minerals, the collection of rugs *Raw* was commercialized by Tai Ping in 2019.

an incredible variety of lustres, materials and techniques is much richer than the one I could use in my drawings. So we worked together, with samples that they proposed to me and that I validated and this resulted in very beautiful pieces, a rather incredible result which I did not necessarily expect, using mixtures of materials that I could not have anticipated from my mere drawing. When I go back to my old sketchbooks today, I find them full of magnificent drawings, but they do not really represent objects or pieces of furniture. They remain drawings, even if sometimes I use them as sources of inspiration for elements, details of current projects.

Drawing became important to me at a time when there were more and more projects, and that involved meetings, forming a team. And so I didn't have the time to work in volume, to make models, to correct them - a very long process. At that time, I dreamed of only one thing: having my own workshop. But all I could do was to isolate myself for an hour and a half every morning in a cafe near my Paris studio and fill my sketchbooks...

At that time, from 2005 onwards, your name appears more and more often in the press, and not only specialized publications. Your name, and also (maybe above all?) your image, that of "film star of design" or of a new incarnation of the so-called "French touch". How did you come to terms with this sudden celebrity?

I have always approached things simply and instinctively and often, it is true, a in a rather naive way. Most of the time, what people wanted me to be was not at all what I was. My upbringing, which had at the same time a Catholic, bourgeois streak and another slightly hippy and anarchist tendency, certainly allowed me to feel comfortable in different environments. I have never consciously set out - although I may have been unconsciously tempted - to create a character. That's why all the labels people wanted to "stick" on me were a source of surprise and I found them all completely incongruous.

Although I did not feel the desire to construct a character or even a style, I felt that around me, I was being pushed in this direction, especially by the press,, who always wanted me to define my style, my inspirations, my mentors... I ended up constructing a discourse to satisfy them; I quoted Carlo Mollino, I talked about nature... there was nothing untrue in all that but it soon became a somewhat convenient highway. And there were also my clients who sometimes responded to a project I proposed « I would like something more Noé Duchaufour-Lawrance »... and there I was lost! Even with hindsight, I find it difficult to position myself in a current or a style. I have however asked myself a thousand times the question: "What is Noé Duchaufour-Lawrance?", "What is your universe?", "How do you define yourself?"... and if I have never really found the answers. In reality, it is when I create that I notice the recurrence of certain elements, the permanence of a certain way of approaching and responding to projects. Basically, I think it is freedom that best characterized my work: I could move from one universe to another. I am well aware that this freedom, this ease of adaptation does not constitute a "style", but in a way it is better; it opens up a wealth of possibilities. In fact, I feel as if I have traveled a lot. It is was only later that I felt the need for a place where I could settle down.

So it was this traveler, free and curious, who responded to the call for projects from Paco Rabanne?

Absolutely, it was that guy who turned up, a bit nonchalantly, for an appointment at Paco Rabanne, at the insistence of Cédric Morisset[22] who was my agent. At that time, Frédéric Hubin[23] , who worked at VIA, was in charge of my relations with the press, especially the international press. My agency was growing and becoming structured, but I was frustrated by the fact that I had no real experience in industrial design, with strict constraints and complex specifications. That also explains why I accepted this competition, along with

[22] Consultant, critic and exhibition curator, Cédric Morrisset (born in 1975) accompanied the debut of Noé Duchaufour-Lawrance as his agent in 2005.
[23] Frédéric Hubin (born in 1974) was an art historian and museologist by training. He was responsible for communication at VIA when he collaborated with Noé Duchaufour-Lawrance, between 2005 and 2007.

Sofa *Borghese* (2012) edited by La Chance.

Bookshelf from the *Naturoscopie* series (2006).

my curiosity to discover a new universe. And I was finally chosen with this gold bar which I fully assume. On the one hand, it was an immediate worldwide success[24] and on the other hand I have no reason to reject it: it is a well designed object, well thought out, easy to handle, an object of which I am quite proud. But I have always been bothered by the values that such an object conveys and today I would not be able to imagine an object so remote from what I am today.

With my « goody goody » side, I enjoyed pleasing the client and delivering what was expected of me. I recognize today that this sometimes gave rise to complete failures. The worst part is that I was completely sincere: I found each project interesting, each problem stimulated me to find a solution but I sometimes let myself be overly influenced by the client... I have in mind a cafe in Saint-Tropez or else a restaurant in Gstaadt as examples of these errors. But these were also learning experiences that made me understand that sometimes you have to refuse projects.

Your work is also noteworthy for the variety of materials that you have explored. Among crystal, ceramics, bronze, cork, composite materials and wood, which do you feel closest to?

[24] From its launch in 2008, the new perfume *One million* by Paco Rabanne held for eight months the first place in world sales of perfumes for men.

Wood has, in my opinion, a particular vibration; it has this wonderful dimension which projects you into a unique sensory universe. You feel that it is a living material that appeals to all the senses. Just think of the wonderful smell that hits you on entering a carpentry workshop! Wood is the material that brings me the most comfort, in contrast to metal which is harsh and sharp. Wood is also a material that I like to combine with others… When I met Anne Lhomme[25], artistic director of Saint-Louis, I imagined a collection that is as much concerned with furniture as it is with objects or light. I am referring to the *Folia* collection which pays homage to the know-how of the oldest crystal factory in France while evoking its direct environment, the forest of the Vosges. In certain pieces of this collection, the marriage of crystal with wood makes the crystal less "sacred", in a way stripping it of its aura of prestige.

There was a real turning point in my life. During my studies in Brest, I was fascinated by industrial architecture, concrete, metal. I really enjoyed walking around the commercial port and observing this dark and cold universe. Metal sculpture, which I studied when I arrived in Paris, was in this vein... in tune with this "dark" side of my culture... I

[25] Having graduated from l'Ecole Penninghen in Paris, Anne Lhomme became design director at the manufacture Saint-Louis in 2009.

Yorgo&Co - visual identity for Noé Duchaufour-Lawrance (2011).
Photo : Yorgo&Co

liked coming home from school with my hands blackened by metal dust, my nose numbed by the corrosive smell of welded metal. I have never understood what led me to a softer, more sensual work, which puts the softness of touch before the rigor of the structure. Maybe my stay in Morocco or becoming a father? I do not know. That said, I sometimes notice, in my work, resurgences of this buried passion for industrial architecture and metal structures, such as the *Odyssey* table[26] made at the Sèvres factory or the *Ammonite* shelf commercialized by Meta.

Yet I believe that the design object is not an end unto itself: it can be extended try elements such as words, sounds.The object resonates with the space that surrounds it, it creates an interaction with its user and all this contributes to a living environment. The piece of furniture is a « transmitter » of messages but the fact that it is an object which serves a purpose makes it more accessible than a sculpture or any other artistic object. The names that I give to each of these objects contribute to this possibility of evocation. These names can evoke journeys, places (*Mediteranea, Calanques, Cintra, Mangrove*[27]…) or even suggest moments in life like the

[26] Designed in 2016, the *Odyssey* table is based around a *Ly* vase, an emblematic model of the Sèvres factory, inspired by Asian ceramics in vogue in the 19th century, by adding an anodized aluminum structure which rests on the shoulders of the vase.

[27] *Mediteranéa* lights commercialized by Petite friture in 2016, *Calanque* coffee tables commercialized by Cinna in 2014, *Sintra* sofa commercialized by Ligne Roset in 2018, *Mangrove* table, commercialized by NDL Editions en 2015.

Corvo chairs, edited by Bernhardt design (2010).

Sunday morning desk[28]. With the same idea of presenting the pieces within a coherent environment, I wanted for example my website to have a dimension of sounds that can suggest a volume, a universe for each object, so that its discovery is as immersive as possible. However, I did not want a melody or a rhythm - apart from the rhythm of tools in use - but rather sound environments composed of the real noises of tools and machines that we recorded with Bastian Zeiselmair[29] in the editors' workshops.

> *Your relationship with nature comes across strongly in your work. However, nature often appears through a prism which synthesizes, digitalizes it, and even renders it artificial...*

I held onto, and idealized my childhood memories of Breton landscapes as a way of escaping from my life in Paris. The minerality of the city was very oppressive for me so I was seeking for these moments of contact with nature, whilst knowing that they were a sort of chimera. This quest gave rise to a somewhat strange project: *Marée noire au clair de lune*[30] which also coincided with a time when I realized that the

---

[28] *Sunday Morning* desk commercialized by Ceccotti Collezioni in 2007.

[29] After a first encounter in 2016 during a workshop at the Domaine de Boisbuchet, the German video artist, graphic and sound designer Bastien Zeiselmair collaborated with the studio Noé Duchaufour-Lawrance in 2017.

[30] Set of unique pieces in black Corian, *Marée noire au clair de lune (Black tide in the moonlight)* explored the ambivalence of a natural material, petroleum. This project was shown at the Galerie Pierre Bergé, in Brussels between December 2008 and January 2009.

action of the designer, like any creative action, had a polluting effect. It was a bit of a self-criticism which, at the same time, was sublimated because I also wanted to show how an oil spill could be beautiful and poetic: a journey between the beauty of creating and the darkness of its consequences.

In the same register I could place the *Naturoscopie* project[31]: it clearly refers to nature but there is nothing natural, on the contrary, everything is extremely synthetic with the use of carbon fiber, resins, synthetic paints, digital programming... Here, my goal was to reproduce a natural, primitive emotion, with something synthetic. It was the consequence of a kind of suffocation: no longer having direct access to the material, no longer being in direct contact with the environment, I created a kind of avatar completely disconnected from my source of inspiration.

On the other hand, the object can be inspired more literally from nature: for example the *Borghese* sofa[32]. It comes from a drawing, almost childlike and naive, that I made of umbrella pines in the gardens of Villa Borghese. I was discovering Rome and I was amazed by the forms of their branches and I filled pages and pages of my sketchbook with these forms.

[31] The *Naturoscopie* collection designed for the Galerie BSL, Paris included kinetic lights, bookshelves and a coffee table all inspired by the natural world. Each piece is in a limited series. This collection was shown for the first time in 2012, in the gallery space for which Noé Duchaufour-Lawrance had just signed the interior design.
[32] *Borghese* sofas edited by La Chance in 2012.

Nature, trees and plants, sensual curves... yet the logo you have been using since 2011 to "sign" your creations is a square, filled with straight lines...

At the start it was Yorgo[33] who forced my hand a bit. Instinctively I had ideas for a rather fluid logo and I had imagined something close to the "infinity" sign. But Yorgo proposed this idea of sticks which, by a kinetic effect draw an « N », creating a movement with rigidity. And in fact, it totally suits me, I am someone who needs a framework, a structure. Indeed whenever I have wanted to create spaces of freedom, there was a part of me that always imposed structures, constraints. Although it is basically not my nature, I need a framed, tidy space. (It is not me but I need it.) So in the end, this logo corresponds pretty well to who I am and to this duality in my work. The curves, the sensuality... but these, let's say "flexible" forms are always tense and structured. Perhaps the legacy of my father who rejected the certainty of a scientific career to become a sculptor? Or maybe also the education received from his mother, my grandmother, a woman whom I adored; with her very strict character, she organized, structured everything.

[33] Yorgo Tloupas (born in 1974), trained at the Penninghen school in Paris and is a graphic designer and artistic director.

And yet we find in your work travail pieces with a calmer, more controlled design... I am thinking especially of those designed for the American editor Bernhardt for example. How can an editor influence a drawing, a form?

The collaboration with Bernhardt has been very fruitful for me, but what is most interesting is that there is a lot of control, and it starts with our relationship itself, which is different from what I share with Ceccotti, where our relationships are, let's say, more "Mediterranean". With Jerry Helling[34], our relationship is more cerebral and when we started to work together, we both agreed that, every year, in Milan, there were too many chairs and that our ambition was not necessarily to add more. So, inevitably, you control your drawing, you put it in a very strict framework. And the *Corvo* armchair[35] reflects that perfectly. It's a generous curve but it's just the line of a pencil. Above all, when I was working on it I was all the time conscious of the fact that we nearly always apprehend a chair from behind and that therefore the back had to be very carefully designed: its structure, like the muscles in an anatomical study, is therefore visible on the back. This restraint is found in certain pieces designed for

[34] Jerry Helling is the president and artistic director of Bernhardt Design, American editor of contemporary furniture created in 1983 within the Bernhardt Furniture Company, important and former (1883) American furniture manufacturer based in North Carolina.
[35] *Corvo* armchair edited by Bernhardt in 2010.

Cinna, such as the *Inside World* desk, whose structure is very pure, or even the pieces in the *Estampes* series[36].

> *Maybe it is to feel less constrained that you decided to commercialize some pieces of furniture yourself, within the structure NDL Editions.*

In fact, most of these pieces are private orders for which I have been able, with the agreement of the sponsor, to retain the publishing rights. For the moment all these pieces exist in a single edition, the sponsor's, but they will constitute the "catalogue" of NDL Editions which I hope to launch in a few months. Despite their sometimes obvious differences (for example between the *Jon* sofa and the *Refine* desk[37]), it's interesting to see how these pieces respond to each other and how they have a certain sensibility in common despite being attached to an individual project, sponsor and to a particular context. They all set out to tell a story with a minimum of signs. But I do not restrict myself either in the materials or in the techniques used. They are pieces that I could not not develop with the editors with whom I usually collaborate and they are for the most part handcrafted in French workshops.

[36] *Inside world* desk and collection of *Estampes* storage furniture. edited by Cinna in 2014.
[37] *Jon* sofa designed for the apartment of an American client in 2017 (architect: Annabelle Selldorf) and *Refine* desk designed for the Parisian residence of a business owner in 2017 (architect: Pierre Yovanovitch).

Carlos Lima building the 'soenga' for the first "Made in Situ" collection (2020). Photo: Noé Duchaufour-Lawrance.

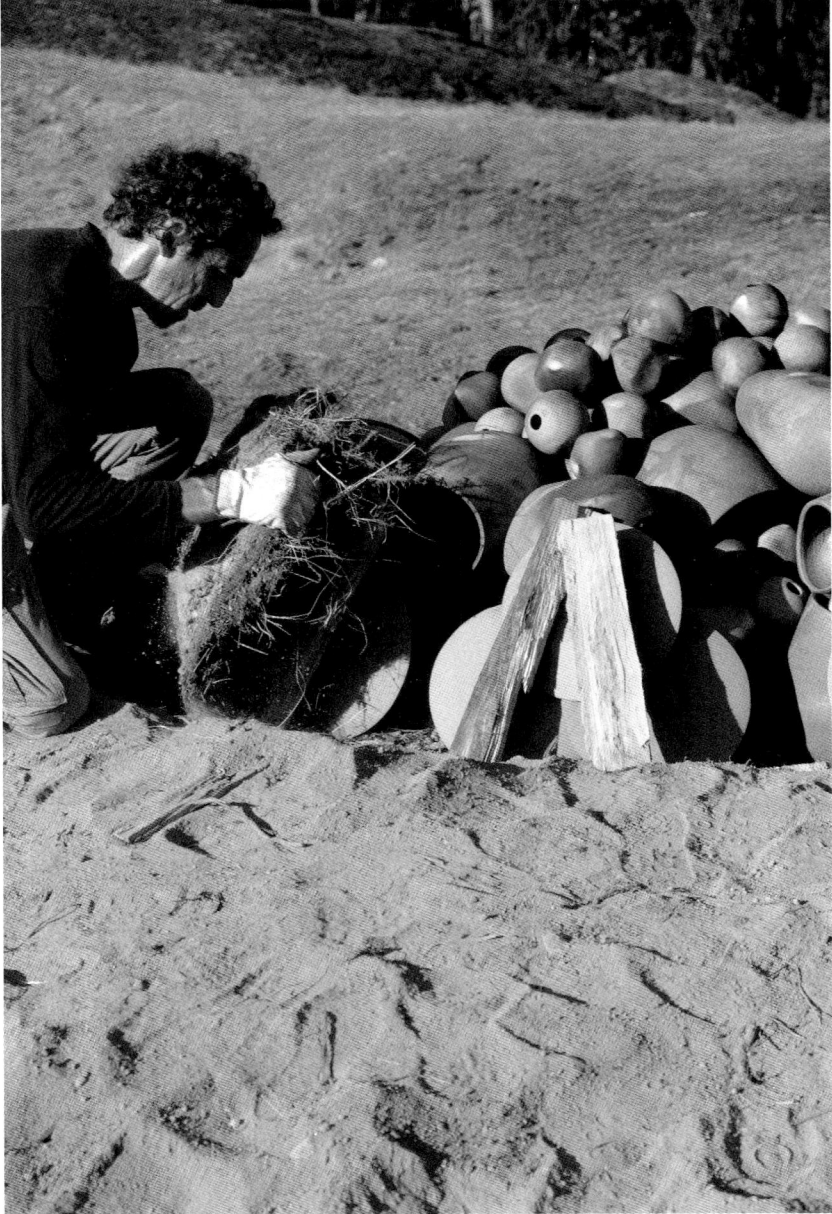

Caractère, a collection de tableware designed for Revol represents a turning point in your work. It came out just at the particular moment in your life when you decided to leave Paris.

In fact, I had been trying to escape Paris for all that time, without really knowing how, but, apart from escaping the city itself, it was also a way of working that I wanted to get away from. At that time I had several quests: I dreamed of space, of being connected to nature and having my own workshop... I realized that I had gradually moved away from all that: I lived in Paris, in this mineral city, in a never-ending round of appointments and with one project after the other.

I then imagined a project, which I called *In Situ* and which was inspired by chefs and friends like Alexandre Gauthier, Armand Arnal or Jean-Denis Lebras[38] who cooked with local resources they found in their immediate vicinity. When I observed them, I realized that in the design sector, very often, we were assembling elements that were made around the world and I wanted to get closer to something more real and more local and above all, more connected to what I had

---

[38] Alexandre Gauthier (born in 1979) is chef and owner of the "Maison de Cuisiniers", La Grenouillère, a two-star restaurant that works with local products. Armand Arnal (born in 1979) created in 2006 in Arles "La Chassagnette", a reputed restaurant located in the center of his vegetable garden. Jean-Denis Lebras (born in 1976) has been Pierre Gagnaire's right-hand man since his apprenticeship in Brest. As such, he was chef of the *Sketch* from 2008 onwards.

known as a child, in Aveyron or in Brittany. We got by with what our direct environment offered us. And so, I studied the possibility of creating such a project, based around a territory. In the Bay of Somme, in the Camargue... I was looking for a place that could bring together chefs and designers to work together in a given territory. The plan was written, thought out, and I had found a financier, David Barry, an American friend who had accompanied me on some exploratory trips to find places. As the project took shape, I realized that in fact, all this complex project was just a way for me, personally, to find a way out, to escape from Paris. And so I abandoned the project until one day when I left, with no particular plans.

One winter, on my way back from Brazil where I had been kitesurfing, I found myself stranded with my family in Lisbon for a few days. I discovered this city around the New Year. I realized that there was no question, this was where I wanted to live. Three months later, in April 2017, I moved there. *Caractére*, it is true, is at a crossroads. It was started in Paris and it was finished when I had recently moved to Portugal. It was also the first time that I started to have confidence in my drawing, the presence of my hand in an economy of signs. The project was not obvious at the start. I was invited to design a collection for the 250th anniversary of Revol, this business with a remarkable know-how, marked by the enormous success of its crumpled cup[39]... In this project, my line is extremely calm, clear, my pencil did exactly what I wanted it to do. For me, the design is the expression of the serenity I felt when I had interiorized my choice, that of leaving for Portugal and freeing myself from a maximum of constraints. And it's also a project that reconnects me to materials and craftsmanship. Revol understood that, because *Caractère* gives pride of place to the raw material; by removing the enamel on the edge of the pieces, the blackness of the earth is revealed and the imperfection of the line is highlighted, the roughness and the uncertainties of a craft industry. They are also dense, massive pieces... I also had in mind the memory of the stoneware plates from my childhood, the plates that were found on farm tables, or that could be found in a monastery! Besides the design of this collection, Revol also asked me to work on the images that would accompany its release. So I imagined a film that explains *Caractère* in addition to the photographs. It was the first time that I was responsible for an entire project, from the design of the object to its communication, in a very simple way and with total confidence.

[39] Established in the department of the Drôme, this family business specializing in culinary earthenware for professionals took on a new lease of life under the impetus of Olivier Passot at the turn of the 2000s by launching a crumpled cup in white earthenware imitating disposable plastic cups. The immediate, massive and worldwide success of this object marked the opening of a new era for the company.

Let's come back to before you left Paris, and your Parisian apartment, which we discover in a well-known interior decoration magazine[40]. One object seems not to fit in the flexible, curved and comfortable environment that you imagined: an Eventail *table[41] designed by Charlotte Perriand, which is an assembly of rectilinear wooden slats. Why this choice ?*

This table is really interesting. In fact, it creates a disturbance in the room because we don't really know how to apprehend it, where to put it, and it gives rise to some quite special mealtimes. It is not strictly speaking an "organic" form because it is made up of straight lines, but on the other hand it develops its own very fluid presence: it imposes its own space, it does not allow itself to be "framed" easily, you cannot install it parallel to a wall, for example. That's what I liked about this table, which, by the way, has followed me to Lisbon. While we are on the subject of Charlotte Perriand, it's strange because, what she did in Japan[42], more than 80 years ago, is in a way the same quest we are continuing today, with the project *Made in Situ* that I set up in Portugal in 2018.

[40] *A family house with a view of Paris* AD France, March 2018, by Sophie Pinet. Photo Alexis Armanet.
[41] Designed by Charlotte Perriand in 1972, it is now published by Cassina
[42] Invited by the Japanese Ministry of Commerce and Industry, Charlotte Perriand went to Japan in 1940. For two years, she accompanied Japanese master craftsmen in order to imagine with them objects that correspond to the modernity which was developing in the world.

Can you elaborate on that ?

The idea behind *Made in Situ* is to discover a country through its crafts, the people who practice them, the materials and resources that make up the territory. I spent my first year here in Portugal thinking about what I wanted to do here. For this break represents a desire to give my work a new direction. Portugal appeared as the ideal place for this project which had been at the back of my mind for years, a place where it could take on a lighter form, more in line with my personality.

With my Portuguese team we spent a year identifying techniques, craftsmen and ressources which could be the basis of projects. We met craftsmen and entered into a dialogue with them and sometimes it went no further than that. Those projects which did take form took a long time. We have to get to know each other to see if there is any prospect of working together. For *Made in Situ*, there are no preparatory drawings and no preconceived ideas before the meetings. With these craftsmen I have no pedigree, I do not exist, there is no a priori but there are also no expectations. It can be very laborious and sometimes we come up against a refusal. The craftsmen don't necessarily want to get out of their usual way of doing things, or it can be due to a sort of apprehension. In fact, in Portugal, anything connected to craft industry was denigrated for years following the régime of Salazar. There was a desire to industrialize the country as quickly as possible.

At the same time, the affirmation of the identity of the country during the dictatorship was closely tied to the development of folklore. That explains why after the Revolution of the Carnations, craft production with a "folk" feel to it was often associated with a somewhat nationalist conservatism. Today's artisans still live with this ambivalent heritage which can also explain their reaction.

The name of this project is *Made in Situ*. It is a sort of mobile project on the scale of Portugal. We could have used a caravan to meet all these people but we opened our base in Lisbon[43] which is intended as a showroom where the objects produced during these collaborations will be presented and sold, but which will also house my studio and a large kitchen. The first project that we will present will be devoted to "barro negro"[44]. It is a technique whereby clay objects are cooked directly in the ground. The objects are placed in a pit dug in the ground, they are covered with peat and the fire is lit. The firing takes place in a "smothered" way and the lack of oxygen inside this makeshift oven, causes the oxidation of the clay which turns black. The process has something of alchemy about it. It's

[43] The address is Travessa do Rosario 15 in the Principe Real district.

[44] Initially discovered in Mexico, the technique of "barro negro", black pottery, is still a living craft in Bisalhães and Tondela in Portugal. Transmitted almost exclusively within families, the practice is threatened by the decline in the number of practitioners, the lack of interest in the younger generations and competition from industrial products. In 2016 this technique was inscribed on the list of intangible heritage requiring urgent safeguarding by Unesco.

amazing to find techniques here that are also found in Latin America or Eastern Europe, for example. The first series of objects that I will present will be the result of this technique involving two master ceramists, Xana Monteiro and Carlos Lima, from Moleos, a village in the north of Portugal. The potters of neighboring villages organize annually a "soenga", a collective firing. Thanks to the whole-hearted participation of Xana and Carlos, we organized our own "soenga", next to their workshop. Rarely have I experienced such strong vibrations during the production of my own objects. The result was less important than the firing itself, in which a certain alchemy seemed to be at work. The fire of the "soenga" is hard on the pieces and imposes its own rules. It is impossible to predetermine the result. This unique experience created objects which seem to have a life of their own.

This project is deeply rooted in a territory, and in the history of those who live there and that is exactly what I was searching for in Portugal.

In our showroom, in Lisbon, the work of these artisans will be highlighted but I also want the kitchen to be used by chefs who continue the exploration of the territory by finding the gastronomic resonances of the terroirs where the artisans come from. That provides the link with my first vision of « in Situ » which I had in France.

The relation between the object and its surrounding space is also a central element in this project. Each collection of objects will have its own scenography, and for that I rely on the work of an old friend, the scenographer Clémence Farrel.

After "barro negro", I plan to work on cork. When I arrived in Portugal in 2017, I crossed the country by car, transporting fa lot of my family's belongings. A great fire had been ravaging the country and I found myself on roads in the middle of a lunar landscape. This terrible and strangely beautiful image still haunts me. I took a lot of photos of this landscape full of charred trees, cork oaks... Since then, I have met a cork manufacturer with whom we will make pieces of furniture from charred cork . Then it will certainly be bronze, with a manufacturer who normally manufactures propellers for boats, then later, "bunho" (a braided vegetable fiber), marble…

As I progress in this project, I realize that in my work I need these roots, this anchoring. I thereby create for myself constraints that arise from the context, the tools, the material and which allow me to go into a variety of materials and therefore forms.

All this represents a lot of effort and work… but that corresponds to my feeling for Portugal which goes beyond the good life, the beach, the sun… to recognize that it is a country that is not always hospitable, or comfortable. Portugal is a country whose confidence must be won every day. Portugal is cold in winter, it is the raging ocean, it is the jagged coast.

It is a sort of Finistère.

Portugal's Coast.
Photo: Noé Duchaufour-Lawrance

(*clockwise*)
Noé Duchaufour-Lawrance et his mother, Odile Duchaufour (1976) - The Lacombe house, Saint-Laurent-d'Olt, Aveyron- Bertrand Bougé, Lacombe (1974) - Sculpture by Bertrand Bougé.

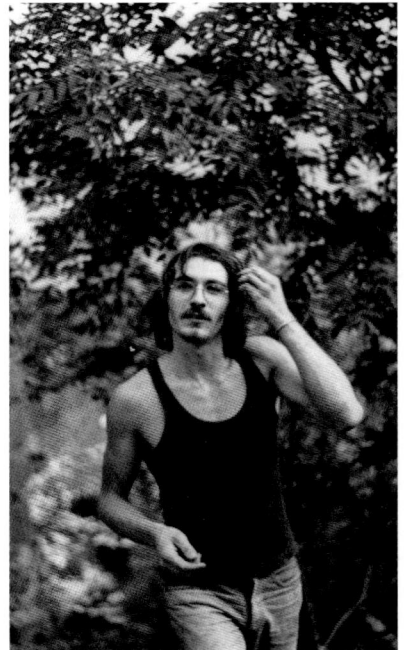

(*clockwise*)
Sculptures by Bertrand Bougé, Lacombe - Lacombe house entrance door -
Odile Duchaufour in the Lacombe house (1976).

(*clockwise*)
Noé Duchaufour-Lawrance in a black-smith workshop, Aveyron (circa 1980) - Brian Lawrance (circa 1980) - Ron Arad, This *Mortal Coil* Bookshelf (1993) edited par One/Off.

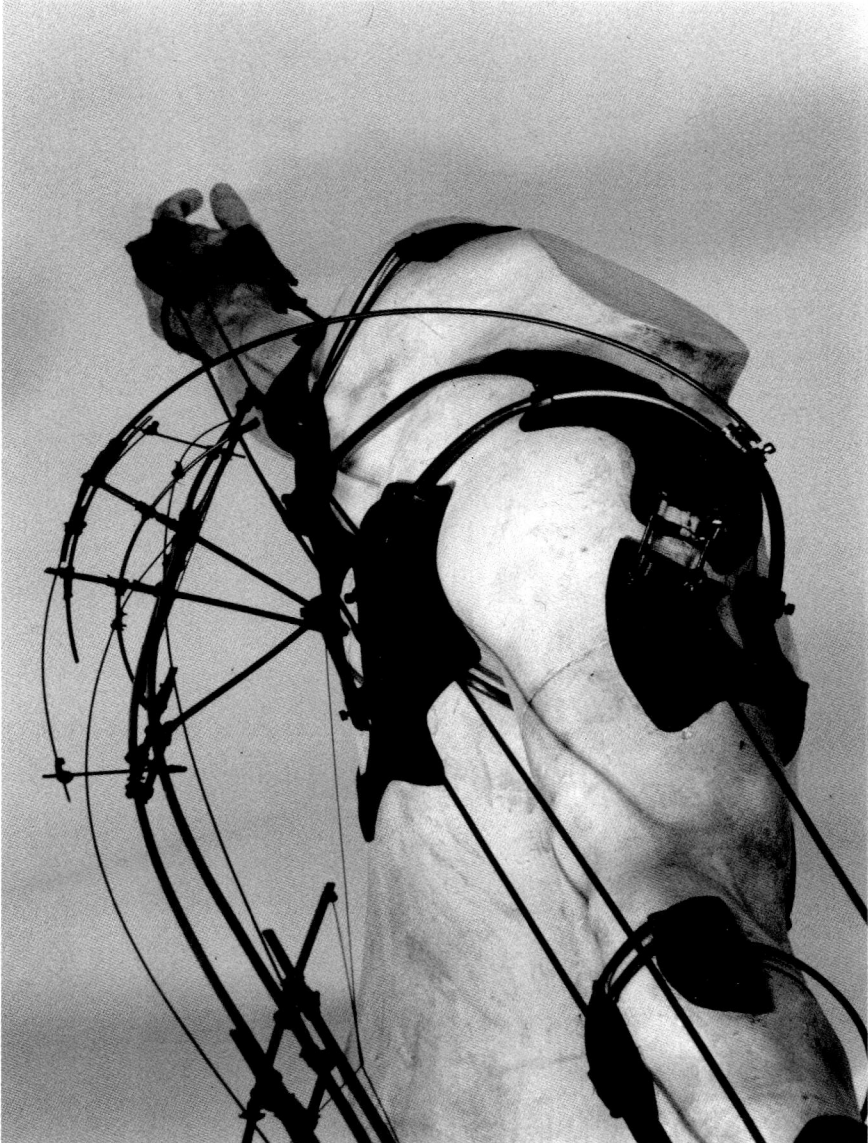

Corps Structure, sculpture by Noé Duchaufour-Lawrance (circa 1992).

Corps Structure, sculpture by Noé Duchaufour-Lawrance (circa 1992).

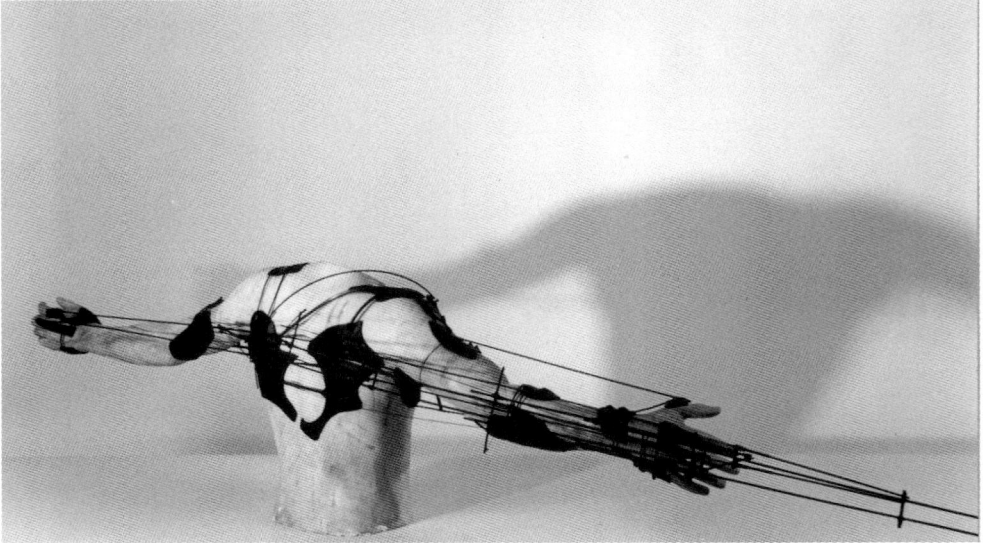

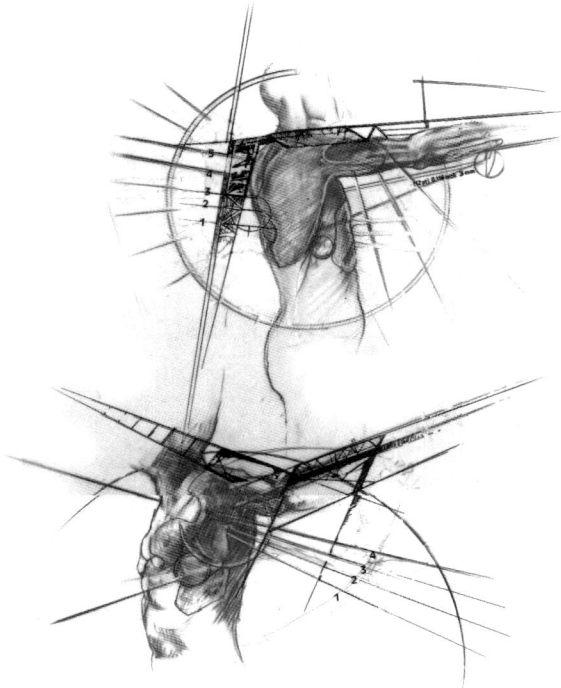

Study for *Corps Structure*,
Noé Duchaufour-Lawrance master's project for ENSAAMA Olivier de Serre school (circa 1992).

Stretched canvas table by Noé Duchaufour-Lawrance (1995) in the ENSAD school hall, Paris.

1 ▶

◄ 3

◄ 4

◀ 6

8 ▶

◀ 10

9 ▶

◀ 11

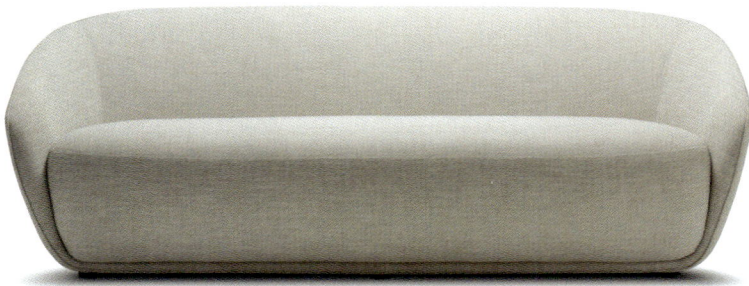

◀ 12

14 ▶

15 ▶

16 ▶

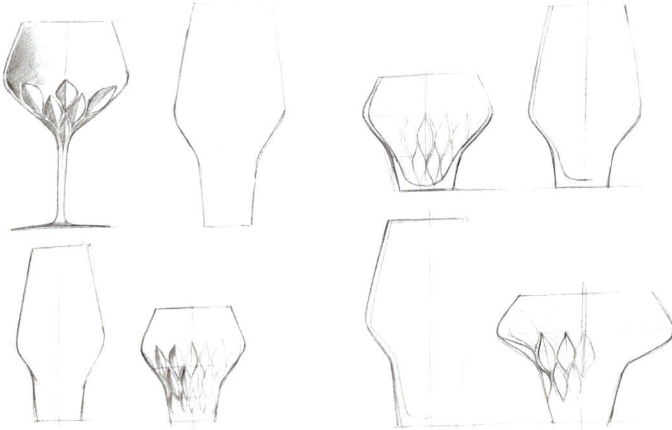

17 ▶

18 ▼

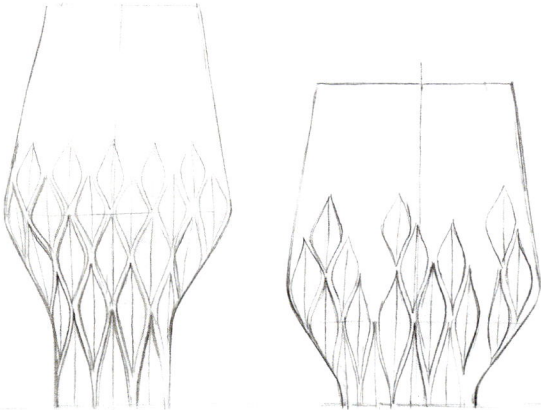

19 ▼

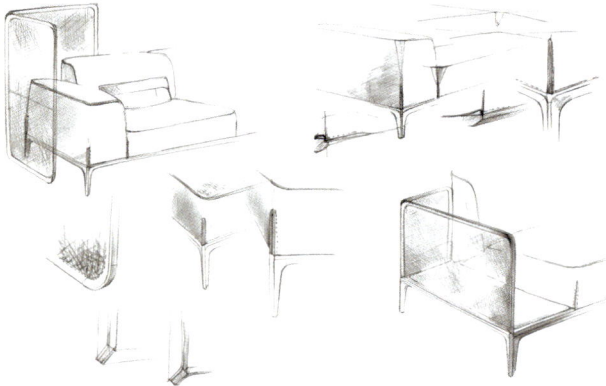

◀ 20

23 ▼

▼ 24

◄ 25

◀ 28

29 ▶

30 ▶▶

31 ▶

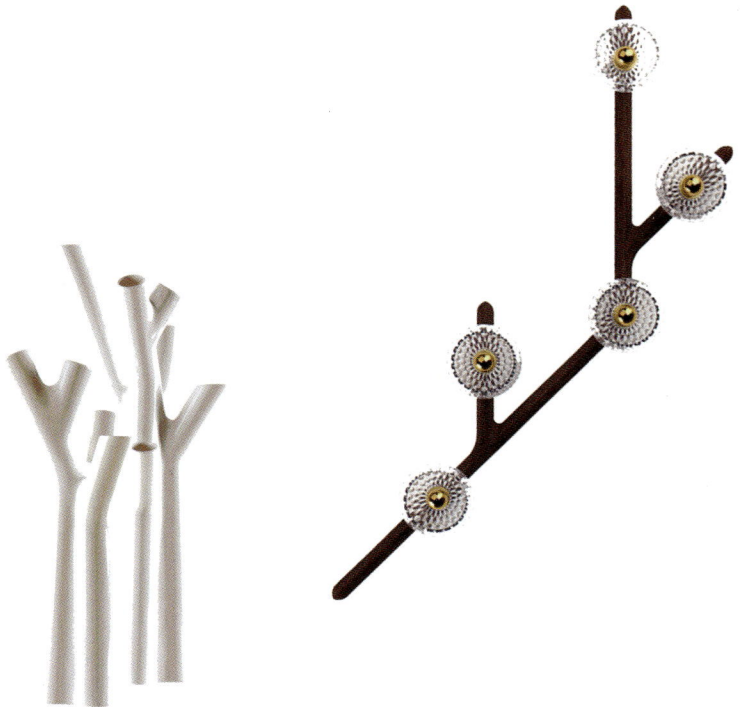

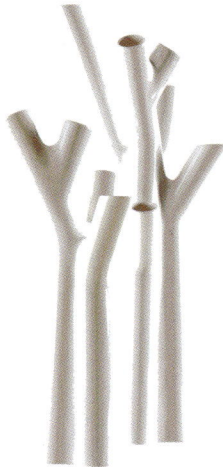

◀◀ 34

NOÉ DUCHAUFOUR-LAWRANCE was born on July 25, **1974**, at Mende, in Lozere. He earned his Baccalaureate F12 diploma at the Kerichen High School, in Brest, studied metal sculpture at the National School of Applied Arts and Crafts, and then design at the Paris National School of Decorative Arts.

His career began at the turn of the **2000**'s, with the delivery of the *Sketch* restaurant in London, for which he earned, among other honours, the prize for Best Design awarded by Time Out magazine (2003).

In **2003**, he designed the *Senderens* restaurant in Paris.

In **2005**, he edited his first pieces of furniture for the Italian publishers, Zanotta and Ceccotti Collezioni, and designed the interior of the *3rd Culture* boutique in Tokyo.

In **2006**, the *Manta* office collection, the result of his research during his training at the National School of Decorative Arts, was presented by Ceccotti Collezioni.

2007 saw the creation of the *Sunday Morning* office with Ceccotti, but above all the delivery of major interior design projects, including the *Air France Lounge* at Narita airport, in Tokyo. That same year he completed the refurbishment of the *Café Sénéquier* in St. Tropez and the *Maya Bay* restaurant in Monte Carlo. He was named "Designer of the Year" at the Salon Maison & Objet, Paris.

2008 Paco Rabanne entrusted him with the design of his new men's fragrance, *One Million*. He collaborated with Chevallier, for whom he conceived his first *Confluence* carpet, and with Longchamp, for whom he designed the *Landscape* desk set. He continued his collaboration with Ceccotti Collezioni, which presented the *Buonanotte Valentina bed that year.*

In **2009**, the following year, this bed won the Wallpaper Design Awards. That same year he collaborated again with Zanotta (*Derby* armchair) and conceived the ensemble, *Marée noire au clair de Lune* for the Pierre Bergé gallery in Brussels. He also began his collaboration with Ligne Roset by designing the *Roseau* vase.

2010 marked the beginning of his work for the American publisher, Bernhardt Design, for whom he designed the *Corvo* chair, which was honoured with the "NeoCon Gold Award". Paco Rabane commissioned him to design the women's version of *One Million, Lady Million.* He also edited the *Ottoman* seating series for Cinna, the *Cala* armchair for Zanotta, and delivered the interior design for the BSL Gallery in Paris, which served as a showcase for the presentation of *Lucy*, a precious object and organic jewelry holder created for the occasion.
He also designed a serving table for Perrier-Jouët champagne.

In **2011**, he received a "Red Dot Award" for his *Corvo* armchair, presented by Bernhardt, and continued his collaboration with Chevallier by designing the *Plis seat mat.* He returned to interior design by designing the chalet, *La Transhumance*, located in the Alps, and which is the subject of many publications in decoration magazines. He also designed the architectural concept for the Yves Saint Laurent perfume stands. For the publisher Saint Luc, he explored the work of linen fibre with the *Duales* table.

In **2012,** the first limited edition work, the *Naturoscopie* collection, was presented at the BSL gallery. For the young French publishers, La Chance and Marcel, respectively, he created the *Borghese* sofa and the *Bambi* chair. While the *Monk* coffee table is manufactured by Pleyel and the *Ammonite* shelf by Meta, Noé Duchaufour-Lawrance delivered three important interior design projects: the *Air France Business Lounge* at Charles de Gaulle airport (in association with Brandimage), the *Yquem* private tasting room at the restaurant of the Hotel Meurice in Paris, and the Ciel de Paris restaurant, located on the 56th floor of the Montparnasse Tower.

In **2013**, GQ magazine named him "Best Designer of the Year". He was invited to Thomas Erberet's curiosity cabinet, where he designed a unique version of the *Market Chair*, a product stamped Petite Friture, which marked the beginning of their collaboration.
He unveiled his first glass pieces (*Fusion*, *Flux* and *Babel* lighting fixtures) under the Gaia&Gino label, while Kundalini presented the *Peacock* and *Forestier*, *East* suspension lamp.

In January **2014**, the cutler Perceval invited Noé Duchaufour-Lawrance to create a knife - *Le Noé*, and the Maison & Objet trade show asked him to design the scenography of its *Scène d'Intérieurs* space, a collaboration that would be repeated in future editions.
Cinna's catalogue was enriched by four series of his furniture: *Calanque* coffee tables, *Inside World* desk, *Kiji* table and *Estampe* storage units. At Bernhardt, the *Harper* rocking chair and the *Cinema* seating collection were presented. Seating is also in the spotlight with Italian collaborators, Zanotta with the *Arom* Armchair and Tacchini with the *Shelter* Armchair. That same year, inspired by the project of the restaurant *Ciel de Paris*, he developed an eponymous chair with the French publisher Tabisso, who produced a collection.
Distinguishing his work in interior design, the magazine AD invited Noé Duchaufour-Lawrance to present in the exhibition "ADIntérieurs", organized at the Museum of Decorative Arts.

2015 the *Ciel!* chair was consecrated by the Via label.
The *Mangrove* table, self-edited and presented by Thomas Erber in his curiosity cabinet, comes out of Neal Feay's Californian workshops.

In **2016**, these same workshops collaborated in the manufacture of the Odyssey table, designed for and with the Sèvres National Manufactory. This house invited him to lead a workshop around the theme of gesture and excellence for 3rd year students of the Decorative Arts. That year, Duchaufour-Lawrance signed a new architectural concept for the Montblanc boutiques, which is to be applied worldwide, and participated in the rehabilitation of the *#cloud.paris building* by designing the lounge. He also designed a collection of *Mediterranea* lighting fixtures for Petite Friture, and unveiled the T*ransmissions* collection, pieces unveiled at the Gobelins gallery, as part of a "Carte blanche" for the Mobilier national. It consisted of a desk, two seats and a storage unit that mobilized the expertise of the ARC, the institution's research and creation workshop. Continuing his collaboration with Bernhardt Design, Noé Duchaufour-Lawrance added seven new pieces to his catalogue, including the *Clue* and *Chance* coffee tables and the *Modern Family* collection, which was decorated with the "NeoCon Silver Award".
Also in **2016**, Hermès added the S*ellier* sofa to its furniture catalogue.

In **2017**, the Chinese publisher Zaozuo added the *Belle Ile* sofa to its catalogue. That same year, *Folia*, a collection of 25 pieces (furniture and lighting) developed for the Saint-Louis crystal factory, was introduced. A few private arrangements offered Noé Duchaufour-Lawrance the opportunity to create new pieces that join the NDL Editions catalogue, such as the *Camino* carpet, the *Jon* seats, the *Milo* tables, the *Collar* side table and the *Refine* desk. These pieces allowed him to establish a dialogue, a close and privileged collaboration with exceptional French manufacturers.

In **2018**, coinciding with its discovery and installation in Portugal, Ligne Roset presented the *Sintra* sofa. It released the *Aqua* surfboard and presented the *Character* china collection for the porcelain maker Revol.

In **2019**, selected to design custom furniture for a prestigious Middle Eastern client, for whom he created workspaces, furniture and precious accessories, most of which were added to the NDL Editions catalogue. The carpet publisher Tai Ping presented a collection of eight carpets entitled *Raw* and the Saint-Louis house, a sequel to the *Folia* chandelier collection, at the Milan furniture fair.

2020. Dividing his time between his Parisian and Lisbon studio, Noé Duchaufour-Lawrance developed *Made in Situ* in Portugal: a self-published program of exclusive collections of furniture and objects featuring design and local craftsmanship to the rhythm of the seasons. *The Made in Situ* presentation and reception area - opened in September - also aimed to create occasional bridges with other disciplines dear to the designer, from gastronomy to music, among others.

2021 is a year that will mark the launch of a line of furniture for La Manufacture and glass coffee tables with the Punta Conterie gallery in Venice. His sensitivity for local craftsmanship found an echo with the young publishing house Maison Intègre, for which he designed bronze pieces that were then shaped using the ancestral techniques of craftsmen from Burkina Faso.
Carried by the Hermès Corporate Foundation, the 5th edition of the Academy of Craftsmanship, this year - 2021 - dedicated to glass and crystal, will be placed under the educational direction of Noé Duchaufour-Lawrance.